LOTS AND LOTS OF ZEBRA STRIPES

PATTERNS IN NATURE

WRITTEN AND PHOTOGRAPHED BY

STEPHEN R. SWINBURNE

HOUGHTON MIFFLIN BOSTON

Foreword

Everywhere you go, you can find patterns in nature. They can be up in the clouds, or down in the sand. You might see a pattern in a cat's fur, a bird's feather, or a butterfly's wing. Some patterns are big like rainbows and some are small like a spider's web. You can even find a pattern in your favorite snack — a pineapple or watermelon. Once you begin to see the circles, stripes, and spirals in nature, you will find patterns in lots of places.

Many patterns have a purpose. The rings of a tree tell its age. The stripes on a garter snake act as a disguise. His pattern helps him hide. And many patterns are just beautiful to look at — the ripples on a pond, the frost on a window, or the piles of soap bubbles at bath time.

Certain patterns are unique. Did you know that no two snowflakes are alike? Did you know that no two zebras have the same pattern of stripes and no two giraffes have the same pattern of dark patches?

You may have seen some of the patterns in this book before, while some may be new. If you visit the zoo or go to a park, beach, or pond, it's fun to go on a pattern hunt. How many patterns can you find right outside your door?

— Steve Swinburne

Patterns are lines and shapes that repeat.

Some patterns are simple and some are not.

You can find patterns in

spring,

summer,

fall,

and winter.

Patterns can be circles or spots.

Patterns can be stripes or lines.

Patterns can be spirals.

Patterns can be found on the fur of animals

or the feathers of a bird.

Patterns can be found on the scales of a snake

or the shell of a turtle.

Some patterns show growth.

Some patterns show age.

Some patterns are straight lines.

Some patterns are curved lines.

You can find patterns in a park,

on a pond,

at a beach,

or on the forest floor.

Finding a pattern is fun.

Look for patterns where you live.

Can you find patterns in your lunch snack?

Can you find patterns on shells?

Can you find patterns in vegetables?

Can you find patterns on insects?

Can you find patterns on trees?

Can you find patterns on flowers?

Patterns make our world a beautiful place.

Discover Science!

Science is observing.

Science is sorting and classifying.

Science is recording.

Science is sharing your discovery!

Math 123 LINK

Animal Parade

Look at these five animals!

Which one is first in line?

Which one is last?

Which one does not have a pattern?

Zebra

Zebra.

Zebra.

Which is right —

White on black —

Or black on white?

by Langston Hughes